A LOVE AND IT

explorations of T.S.Eliot

Christopher Southgate

UNIVERSITY OF SALZBURG

Salzburg - Oxford - Portland

First published in 1997 by **Salzburg University** in its series:
SALZBURG STUDIES IN ENGLISH LITERATURE
POETIC DRAMA & POETIC THEORY
179

EDITORS: WOLFGANG GÖRTSCHACHER & JAMES HOGG
INSTITUT FÜR ANGLISTIK UND AMERIKANISTIK
UNIVERSITÄT SALZBURG
A-5020 SALZBURG
AUSTRIA

British Library Cataloguing in Publication Data:

Southgate, Christopher, 1953-
    A Love and its Sounding: explorations of T.S.Eliot. -
(Salzburg studies in English literature, poetic drama &
poetic theory ; 179)
    1.Eliot, T. S. (Thomas Stearns), 1888-1965 - Criticism and
interpretation 2.Eliot, T. S. (Thomas Stearns), 1888-1965 -
In literature 3.Poets, English - 20th Century - Biography
I.Title
821.9'12

ISBN 3705200984

Foreword © Anne Stevenson 1997
All other text © Christopher Southgate 1997

Christopher Southgate is hereby identified as author of this work in accordance with section 77 of the Copyright Designs and Patents Act 1988.

Cover design: Adam Denchfield Design. Consultant: Bee Willey

Typeset in Bembo. Printed & bound by E.J.Rickard Ltd, Cattedown, Plymouth.

Distributed by:
Drake International Services
Market House, Market Place
Deddington
Oxford OX15 0SF
England
Phone 01869 338240
Fax: 01869 338310

Distributed in the U.S.A. by
International Specialised
Book Services Inc.
5804 NE Hassalo St
Portland
Oregon 97213-3644
Phone 503.287.3093
Fax: 503.280.8832

CONTENTS

Acknowledgements   4

The poem: 'A Love and its Sounding'

    Author's Note   6

    Foreword by Anne Stevenson   7

    I   10

    II   16

    III   24

    IV   34

    V   46

    VI   54

    VII   62

Three essays:

    I - Bleistein derided: Eliot and anti-Semitism   75

    II - That she *does* love: Eliot and Emily   81

    III - Calling a Friday good: Eliot and faith   89

Bibliography   95

Acknowledgements

Many poets and scholars have generously given their help and counsel over the six-year genesis of this book. In particular Lyndall Gordon, Jane Beeson, Mark Beeson, Judy Hogan, Matt Simpson, Richard Skinner, Anne Stevenson and Ron Tamplin commented most helpfully on drafts of the poem, and Peter Faulkner made judicious observations on the essays. I am also grateful for certain specific comments by Mrs Valerie Eliot. Any remaining inaccuracies in the work are of course entirely the responsibility of the author.

I thank the Literary Estate of V.A.Demant for permission to quote from his address at the Requiem Mass for Eliot. Brief direct quotations from Eliot's own published work are made for the purposes of constructive critical comment only. For details of their sources see p95.

My researches into Eliot were enormously helped by time spent in the Modern Archive at King's College, Cambridge, working with the John Hayward Bequest. I am grateful to the staff there, and also at the Beinecke Library at Yale. In thanking my former research supervisor Hal Dixon for his introduction to the King's Archive I acknowledge also my debt to his example to me over many years: to the confidence imparted by his wide-ranging academic curiosity combined with utter intellectual integrity, also to his tireless personal kindness.

It is a pleasure to thank those who brought 'A Love' to birth in performance: Richard Burridge for his great enthusiasm and encouragement, also Richard and Anne Eyre, Kay Dunbar and Joy Thompson who arranged the poem's other early readings, and Douglas Dettmer, Rachel Acworth and Richard Skinner for acting as co-readers.

James Hogg at Salzburg has superintended publication with courtesy and efficiency, giving the author the utmost freedom.

My wife Sandy endured all the vicissitudes of a long and eccentric project and has loved me through it – it is to her, with great affection, that the work is finally dedicated.

A LOVE AND ITS SOUNDING

explorations of T.S. Eliot

Christopher Southgate

UNIVERSITY OF SALZBURG

Salzburg - Oxford - Portland

Author's Note

The poem 'A Love and its Sounding' derives its plan from the conviction that a writer who searched continually for religious insight must reveal in his life hints of God's own activity within that life. So T.S.Eliot's life became for me a poetic and theological test-bed, a basis for 'myth-making' (myth here being thought of in the technical sense of the depiction of underlying truths about God and human beings). Eliot's vivid experiences of childhood, suffering and redemption suggested the mythic structure found in the first sections of the Bible, from the Eden story to the return of the Israelites from exile.

The best rationales for imaginative explorations are those one reads after completing the journey. When I had just finished the biographical poem which forms the first part of this volume I read the following:

> Every great man's life illuminates our own. The longer we stay with him, the more we learn from him, the more our own life becomes entangled with his, and through his with a common life of self-transcending scope. We enter through him, insofar as we learn to grow in communion with him, a life at once more charged with human possibilities, more exposed to conflict and contradiction, more rich in resources. (Alan Ecclestone, writing of the French poet Charles Péguy.)

Conflict and contradiction. Eliot was at times anti-Semitic, and at other times insensitive to the offence he had caused (Essay I). He exposed several people who were close to him to a sudden, unexpected distancing, tantamount to cruelty (Essay II). He became and remained a deep religious believer and the architect of great Christian poetry (Essay III).

To explore intimately fragments of a life which has touched greatness is to appreciate very directly the enormous ambiguity attached to human life; those who 'have eyes to see' will want to discern something of the faithfulness of a God who could create, nurture and redeem such a life, and disclose himself through it.

Foreword to the Poem by Anne Stevenson

Human history has always been strange, and twentieth-century history has been so strange that, like an outsize detachable brain, it scarcely today seems to belong to the long evolutionary drift of its body. No western writer was more painfully aware than Thomas Stearns Eliot of the leap history was taking throughout his lifetime into what he viewed as a depersonalized and hideous barbarism, away from the collapsing structures of a past thickly ivied with the achievements of a Eurocentric civilisation, and secured in those institutions, religious and secular, that had appeared to give them enduring validity. In the nineteen-nineties, the ruins of the 'rented house' Eliot evoked in 'Gerontion' are decaying even more rapidly under the plate-glass and steel of a future he would have detested, yet we still read Eliot. Even our smartest, most up-to-date postmodernists who would like nothing better than to blast Old Possum out of memory have to acknowledge his 'greatness', his 'influence' on twentieth-century culture, his 'central position' as a modernist – in short, his stature as the foremost poet of his age. At the same time, it has of late become a gleeful pastime among Eliot's detractors to sabotage his hegemony in the realm of letters by opening fire on the man himself; on, that is, his élitism, his old-fashioned monarchism, his High Church Anglicanism, his putative anti-feminism and especially on what appears to have been an unappealing and today, of course, a politically damaging anti-Semitism. (The latter did not, to my knowledge, infect Eliot's poetry once he had ceased to be the youthful, cynical creator of Bleistein and the "jew" in 'Gerontion'. A case might just be made against him for anti-Semitic references in *The Waste Land*, but nothing so cheap as racism mars his major Christian epiphanies: 'Ash Wednesday', *Four Quartets*, and *Murder in the Cathedral*.)

Christopher Southgate's 'A Love and its Sounding' explores Eliot's nearly lifelong quarrel with himself from a Christian point of view in a poem of unusual skill, honesty and good taste. By honesty I mean that Southgate takes full cognizance of Eliot's weaknesses along with his strengths, conceding that in London during the second decade of the century, while under the spell of Ezra Pound and well before the Holocaust, Eliot 'larded' his 'interiors' with 'rank anti-Semitism/Conventional to the time'; but he acknowledges, too, Eliot's debt to Pound, the poet-maker. By good taste I mean that

Southgate (thank goodness) makes no attempt whatsoever to psychoanalyze his subject or to pontificate on the rightness or wrongness of Eliot's behaviour during his first marriage. The view of Eliot he develops is too long-sighted and at the same time too personal to fall into formulistic language or to apportion blame where there should be understanding. It envisages Eliot's life as a Christian ordeal, a quest for the 'internal country' of God and its meaning as love. I believe Southgate intended 'sounding' in a nautical sense as well as an aural one, and though the poem traces an impassioned pilgrim's progress, the peace achieved at its end resembles Dante's visionary cosmos more than Bunyan's shuffling off of mortal burdens. Southgate also depicts Eliot as a modern Jacob who, betraying the puritanical traditions of his Boston ancestors, departs from his privileged, be-sistered childhood in St Louis to become lost in a contaminated wilderness of sexual threat and hypocritical worldliness. Eliot's prolonged fight with the angel, who in Southgate's poem is transmogrified, for obvious reasons, into four tempters, is dwelt on at length, while his fame as a poet and success as an editor are mentioned only tangentially.

As to the kind of poem this is, it's hard to find a model for 'A Love and its Sounding' either in our time or in the English literary canon. If the text were witty, scurrilous, or preached in rhyming couplets it might have found precedents in Pope or Johnson. In fact, the poem's three-line, roughly nine-syllable stanzas do not rhyme at all, and though the form controls the language and unites the subject, it never accosts the reader with cleverness or attempts a pastiche of Eliot's own writing. The poem's seriousness is a late twentieth-century seriousness, and its mild tone is that of an admirer who, having made his way through his own spiritual waste land, is in a position to talk to Eliot. This talking, for the most part, takes the form of direct address while maintaining a certain formality; its voice preserves a dignified distance between Southgate own 'musings' and the 'you' it creates respectfully, without seeming to take liberties.

Students are sometimes told that the language of poetry is of a special imaginative order, that it is non-propositional or non-expositional; but here is a poem that is made entirely of propositions yet it works very well, both as a poem and a meditation on a poet whose life and work are regarded - I think rightly - as a double-helix of spiritual determination and poetic achievement. There is no need in such a poem to look beneath the knowledge of the work we have got into the psyche we haven't. Southgate wisely confines himself to exploring the Eliot we more or less know already, establishing something like a confidential friendship with him. Writing of Eliot's four tempters, for example, he describes the poet's resistance first to madness, then to power and connivance 'Dressed like yourself in understatement', but gives most time to the tempter 'you know as well as your own/Life'.

> He is in your sense of self-regard;
> He helps you with the chill blandishments
> Of the first tempter. Not you, surely, Tom.
>
> He advises, sweetly reasonable,
> Understanding of your present dilemma,
> In the difficult case of the other two:
>
> What *is* required of the sane husband
> Of hormones deemed mad? Where does prudence
> End, and sheer abuse of power begin?
>
> The soft voice suggests on, most of all
> He gives power to your old power
> To watch yourself, to watch yourself watching.
>
> The agonized poet, hidden by
> The Gioconda smile – that is what
> He wants you to cultivate, idolise.

This seems to be very good writing indeed, particularly since, if done badly, it would certainly condemn itself as the most vulgar type of cheek. Who is this upstart, Christopher Southgate, that he dares to make the spiritual struggles of T. S. Eliot the subject of a thirty-one page poem? And it is, indeed, surprising that 'A Love and its Sounding' is such an absorbing and original piece of work, for all the rules of poetry and criticism say it shouldn't be. Of course, to respond to it one has to be sympathetic to Eliot. Readers who find Eliot's poetry unpalatable or who are unable to empathize with the process of his spiritual self-making won't want to read yet another critique of an élitist, High Church intellectual reactionary. For the rest of us, even if we aren't technically Christians, this scrupulous exploration of the soundings a great poet took, through his poetry, in the course of a difficult life should plumb the depths of our own hidden rivers of spiritual awareness.

Readers familiar with Eliot's work will find the text full of allusions to the poems and plays. Only those allusions which set the chronology of the poem receive an actual note. For sources of biographical information on Eliot's life see the Bibliography on p95.

Thomas Stearns Eliot was born on September 26, 1888, in St Louis, Missouri, the youngest of seven children (of whom only six survived infancy). He was a delicate child, born with a congenital double hernia. His parents, Henry Ware Eliot and Charlotte Champe Eliot (née Stearns), both came of old New England families - Andrew Eliott of East Coker, Somerset had arrived in Massachusetts in 1667.

A LOVE AND ITS SOUNDING

I

Just as the salmon's returning
Supposes the sleek streams of its birth,
Requires the rock-strewn chases, and pools

Remote, leap-hidden, canopied
With branches, penetrable only
By the fierce insistence of instinct,

So our God-search, full of sorrow,
Presumes our origins do cohere
And that unending longings know a source

Which, continuing in hiddenness,
Not less real than air or fire but
More, still suffers us, still sustains.

Here I pursue a poet's story,
Explore a life for signs of searching
Vindicated, prayer as valid.

I begin at St Louis, your birthplace,
Think back along the smart new railroads
To ancestors, Bostonian Eliots –

Into that heritage, in comfort
You were born, Thomas Stearns, seventh child
Of respectability, Charlotte and Henry.

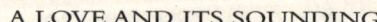

The Revd William Greenleaf Eliot (1811-87) was a formidable figure, who had moved to St Louis in 1834 to further Unitarian and philanthropic work in the area (See Section II).

Jean Verdenal was a French medical student whom Eliot met in Paris in 1910. The two were close friends in the period up to the First World War. Eliot's first book of poems, Prufrock and Other Observations, *bears the dedication "For Jean Verdenal, 1889-1915 mort aux Dardanelles".*

A LOVE AND ITS SOUNDING

The Spirit brooded over Eliots,
With deep, coursing, feminine longing:
Such solid New England stock was not

Easily moved. It gave more weight to
Properly preached wisdom, social standing,
Than to hearts swayed by the great river.

Henry Ware, your father, would have wanted,
His family permitting, to paint:
He managed money, ran a brickmaking works,

Married a woman with poetry
In her fingertips, who might herself,
In other times, have stuck to writing.

Your father's god was the god of *his*
Inexorable, driven father –
Patriarchal, dynastic William Eliot.

Lords walked in the air of your garden,
Yet you would sense that paradise
Drew its life from hidden, sacred wells.

That garden, later so much longed for,
Recollected with Jean Verdenal
On those intense nocturnal Paris walks –

Two men, twenties, driven by thinking
All over the splendid boulevards
Past the ignored doors of gloomy cathedrals

Towards light, a bombardment of choices,
Driven on, talking hard and wildly
Of childhood, past whore-houses, convents;

That was new wine, to talk so freely,
The city full of sudden encounter
With old ironic forms of grandeur -

A great square lined with long dark windows,
A column cased in bronze, from
Cannon melted after Austerlitz -

Full too of alley-shadows, dirt-stained
Slums sloping down towards the river,
And these the more recalled St Louis days,

The welling garden swept by surges,
By memories colliding. Roamed
In search of self, in search of lasting Eden.

Following Section I, 'Eden', the remaining sections of the poem take up in turn the great biblical themes of patriarchs, slavery, exodus, promised land, exile and homecoming.

II

Like Jacob, you were the young son
Of your father's age, born in a house
That remembered your grandfather's journey,

William Eliot's missionary call
From Boston, the Colonies' Ur-place,
West to the wide Mississippi's flood,

To be held there by hot, humid air,
By the river, which baptized both death
And possibility. William built his church,

Founded three schools, a fund for the poor,
A university, in that far
Frontier town, by the yellow mud,

Where ships came with accents of far France,
And copper moons rose on the great stream -
Under the stars of heaven a garden.

Were there those in Ur who felt betrayed?
Faithful friends to Abraham, Fellows
Of the Harvard School of Divinity

Who woke one day to learn that destiny
Called him elsewhere? It is not written.
Only that William carried the line of Eliots

On, stubborn, rich, Unitarian,
Eyes clouded only in death, ending
A driven, implacable sense of duty.

Eliot had not only a strong mother and four older sisters, but also a nurse, Annie Dunne, an Irish Catholic, to whom he was very close in his early years.

The brilliant-red finch <u>Cardinalis Cardinalis</u> is very common in the American South. Eliot later recalled that when his family went back to New England, as they did every summer, he missed 'the long dark river, the ailanthus trees, the flaming cardinal birds...'

The yellow-shafted flicker (<u>Colaptes auratus</u>) is an American woodpecker with brilliant yellow markings on its wings.

The reference here is to Eliot's deep friendship with Emily Hale (see Sections IV-VI, and the second essay in this volume).

A LOVE AND ITS SOUNDING

You must have been born into a house
Still digesting that death, uncertainly.
The youngest, protected by female voices (these

Not yet sinister, nor desperate
Arias of plaintive desire – more
An undemanding chorus of love).

Sistered, you explored, took an interest
In birds, identified their dartings,
Listed songs, made careful observations.

How a cardinal love-feeds his mate
Seed by seed in springtime, but later drives
Her away, rejecting her for weakness.

How a nuthatch sets himself to walk
The face of a hefty trunk of pine –
How days can wear a scarf of wonder

From one bright flash of a flicker's wing
Or the wry intoning of a hundred
Phrases, carpingly, by a mockingbird.

(Did you explain this, many wanders
Later, walking Emily slowly,
Or did fear of losing commend silence?)

Beyond the garden on Locust Street
A fence, a school for young ladies, source
For young Eliots of echoing laughter,

And Tom, daring, precise observer,
Found the door in the fence, found the key,
And after hours explored the empty halls.

19

A LOVE AND ITS SOUNDING

Leah: in the Genesis narrative, Jacob's first wife, whom he did not really love.

Once, your bold fantasies discovered,
The girls were still there, looked down on you,
Laughed for what seemed forever.

After which corridors that had sung
Imagined life, delighted skipping,
Whispered rejection, faintly whined.

If your child-world had always elements
Of solace - its strong love from sisters,
Songs of birds known but fleeting -

These were swept away by necessities:
Growing, being Isaac's Jacob in
Abraham's town, and being a man.

Somehow you amassed inheritance:
Sense of destiny, powers over
Poise and cadence, conviction beyond

Missouri's bounds, and your sweet mother,
Stretching the family mould, pushed you
Onwards. Every inch of the way to Leah.

But I leap over myself to come
To slavery. The child grew among books,
Among ailanthus trees, wisteria,

By twisted trunks of circumstance -
The Hydraulic-Press Brick Company -
Trade, duty, Babel, a mother's ambition.

You were to trace these twists in your mind
As in later trellising of words
You'd trace clematis, tendril and spray,

Eliot's ashes lie in the Parish Church of St Michael and All Angels, East Coker. There is a plaque to mark the place (see Section VII).

After leaving Harvard Eliot travelled in Europe. In 1914 he went to Oxford as part of his doctoral studies in philosophy. After his marriage he became estranged from his father, and he never settled in the US again.

A LOVE AND ITS SOUNDING

Bidding us finally, in complete
Simplicity, in an English church,
Pray for the repose of your soul.

Having drawn so richly on rose and
Twine and thorn. Having been the child of
American promise, who in old age

Became yourself a great patriarch, man
Of many protegés, a critical
Touchstone, a very lion of literature

Who yet had come into his birthright
By a sort of deceit, a slinking
Off to Europe, desertion of Boston

And its rectitudes. Though your father
Blessed you, paid for you, he was to die
When you were thirty, thinking your life a failure.

A LOVE AND ITS SOUNDING

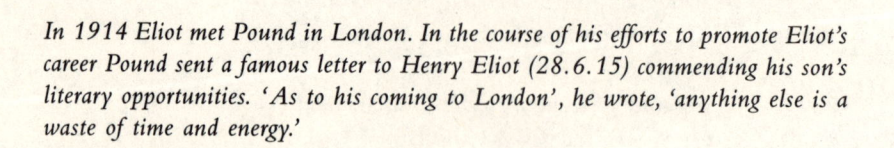

In 1914 Eliot met Pound in London. In the course of his efforts to promote Eliot's career Pound sent a famous letter to Henry Eliot (28.6.15) commending his son's literary opportunities. 'As to his coming to London', he wrote, 'anything else is a waste of time and energy.'

Particularly in poems published in <u>Ara Vos Prec</u> (1920). See the first essay in this volume.

Bleistein: a Jewish character in the poems 'Burbank with a Baedeker; Bleistein with a Cigar', and 'Dirge'.

On June 26, 1915 Eliot married Vivien (sometimes Vivienne) Haigh-Wood, whom he had known only a few weeks. Neither family approved.

III

A new talent needed London; this
Trenchant dictum Ezra Pound, no less,
Expounded to baffled Henry Eliot.

England was the place where clay *could*,
Apparently, be made into bricks
Of poetic reputation. You stayed -

Introduced, encouraged, published at
Pound's behest, trying modernism on myths,
Interiors, martyrs and ladies -

Larding it with the rank anti-Semitism
Conventional to the time, slyly,
In different voices, echoing

The sets you aspired to transcend.
(You had sloughed off your Southern accent
Long since, a snake an unwanted skin -

Assumed instead so easily
Establishment markings: Bleistein
Derided, with eerie savagery.)

You married Vivien, whom your friends
Called 'the river girl'. Lady of scarves,
Quick, frank, glory of an Oxford punting party.

Vivien Haigh-Wood. Mrs T.S.
You had tried the cadences, and had found
They promised a sort of fluency, respectably.

Vivien was of highly nervous disposition and plagued by hormonal problems, including constant menstrual discharge. Incompatibility and illness, physical and mental, dominated their marriage.

A LOVE AND ITS SOUNDING

With Verdenal, in Paris, the streets
Streaming, shining after rain, you'd known
Ideas flow and ripple around your own;

This new current coursed as fiercely,
Had a surface just as bright, the chance
To share, spin stories, gaze at stars,

And underneath miasmatic depths,
Troubling surges. Beyond your boyhood's
Sisterings, clasps, the calling of monsters.

Necessary to poetry, Ezra
Said. The river would teach you dalliance,
Channels new and overflowing, elementals.

The marriage is like a much-planned night
At an exotic restaurant, Thai
Perhaps, or Japanese. Easy to enter,

Comfortable, the powers conspiring
To surround you with delight, everyone
Attentive, the evening long on promise.

And just as you, dandified to a
Degree, ironic as ever, stretch
Yourself into the menu, the drilling starts.

It's outside, of course, peripheral.
You and she are together in the
Idyll you have promised yourselves.

How is it then that the hammer-drill
Is loudest in the most private time –
Dancers gone, bill already sent for?

Leonard and Virginia Woolf published Eliot's work through the Hogarth Press until his move to Faber. Lady Ottoline Morrell held many famous literary gatherings at her country house at Garsington, near Oxford. Eliot had been introduced to her by Bertrand Russell, whom he had met originally during Russell's visit to Harvard (source of Eliot's poem 'Mr. Apollinax'). Russell lent the Eliots money, and for a while they shared a small flat with him. Ray Monk's recent biography of Russell (see Bibliography, p96) charts the course of this three-way relationship. In 1917 Eliot went to work in the Foreign Debt Department of Lloyd's Bank.

A LOVE AND ITS SOUNDING

Your mind is clear, is a rare alloy
Of two countries, of Harvard and Oxford,
And grand and literary weekends.

The hammer-note hits the front of this
Fine head, stops short of unendurable,
Just, but the background whine continues.

In place of the spiritual feast
Vivien and you were to have made
Together, decorously and with passion,

Giving and receiving in ancient
Ritual, solemn joy, throwing across
Sensual shoulders the scarves of evening,

Comes this incessant vibration, this
Static on every wavelength. No
Rapport, no baring of your reticent soul,

Nothing can be sure to be received.
Vivien has a headache, feels sick,
Dislikes the clever Woolfs, your publishers,

Loathes Ottoline Morrell and all
That Garsington lot, makes you take alms
From Bertrand Russell, finds energy to bed him.

By now you are in the Bank, the bricks
You make are from the straw of foreign
Debt. You pay and pay again, and wonder.

'Genius' - Ezra and Vivien
Stress this - going out among millions
Of clerks to chart the profit and loss of war.

See Section IV.

A LOVE AND ITS SOUNDING

A travesty, they say, such a safe
Servitude – security of the
Hollow men. For you a strange haven.

For now you distinguish normality
From the life of the flat, the clinic.
You list debts, Vivien acts the tension.

The more you withdraw in search of peace
The more your wife thrusts feelings at you,
Armfuls of spaniels, fawning and snapping...

Fear of failure mocks at you, through the
Clamour of two self-obsessions, through
Hysterics which leave you no right of reply;

The worst attack your sense, undimmed,
Of being special, called to more than this,
Marked in Missouri for high destiny.

Later this sense would come as the last,
The unexpected tempter. Not yet.
Satan despises those already tortured.

Years trudged in the brown light of winter
London, and that same light, that *Zeitgeist*,
Internalised without relief. The waste.

You would welcome arrows, just one sharp
Shaft of unconsummable love,
One fierce sense of purer spirit.

You deplore, and long for, this distant
Glimpse of *Beatrice*, depict clerks,
Live the keening. Slavery. The sadness.

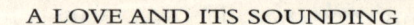

By the autumn of 1921 Eliot himself was in a state of emotional collapse. He went first to Margate and then to Lausanne to recuperate. From Switzerland he sent Pound drafts of The Waste Land, accepting major cuts and revisions.

Various obscene poems Eliot tore from a notebook to give to Pound, featuring characters such as 'King Bolo', are now published as an appendix to Inventions of the March Hare.

A LOVE AND ITS SOUNDING

Waste is the country you make – secret
Aching territory between
Bank and Viv, Virginia, Ottoline.

Something has happened to those, oh so
Elegant thought-mansions built with Jean
Pacing the Ile St Louis, minds attuned.

Some unexplained birdsong has called you
To a dark-towered prison, from which you
Hear water flow unattainably by.

And the task that you find you have set
Yourself is to rebuild this prison
From inside out, in dark satanic brick.

Somehow the internal country must be God's –
Into it you cast wreckage of towers,
Reviling spring and sweet ladies – sirens –

Listening for the unexplained name
On ancient thunder. But Ezra, gleefully,
Seizing on fragmentation, freezing it,

Found you further prizes. Work sent
From the edge of breaking became the
Great Jazz Age rhythmic grumble.

In return for which recasting
You gave Pound your scatological
Scraps – your rude and phallic Bolo –

And the *'miglior fabbro'* of the
Waste Land dedication, the high-point
Of a great collaboration, later to pall.

The baptism was on June 29, 1927 in Finstock Church, Oxfordshire. In the same year Eliot was naturalised as a British citizen. He made his confession to Father Underhill in March 1928.

Charlotte Champe Eliot died in September 1929.

Eliot went to the States in September 1932 to give the Charles Eliot Norton Lectures at Harvard. While he was away he arranged for his solicitor to notify Vivien that a state of separation existed between them.

'Ash Wednesday' was published in 1930. The poem at first carried a dedication to Vivien, which Eliot later withdrew.

IV

There was deliverance, and a long
Wandering at the gates of a land
Promised and forbidden. There was acceptance.

But the details are hidden. There are
Evident only the bare data:
That on such a day you were baptized,

On such a day made your first fateful
Confession. That your dearest female
Anchor dropped away with your mother's passing -

Devoted, misunderstanding you
As ever. And that your Harvard trip
Of 'thirty-two enabled you to leave Viv

By dint of a kind of solicitor's
Nunc Dimittis, blasphemously sung
Over the seedy mansion of her sorrow,

Her mind like a stretched string, plucked and plucked
Again, finally torn from the harsh
Harp of your brilliant tuning.

The desert is a place where Satan
And God are equally close at hand;
A place of turning, seasonless and stark.

Sight-lines are long in the Eliots'
Desert. There is little cover from
The hunting-gaze of pure-white leopards.

As a teenager Eliot sailed every summer off Gloucester, Massachusetts, experience on which he drew in particular in the 'water' <u>Quartet</u>, 'The Dry Salvages'.

The summer he left Harvard Eliot had a sudden mystical experience, profoundly important to him, which he recalled in his early poem 'Silence'.

A LOVE AND ITS SOUNDING

The light is uninterrupted, harsh,
It shrieks off dunes, stone-chutes;
There is little warning of precipice.

Sound. Sound carries a vast, clean distance
Out here, as does the utter silence
Of the Muse, and your wife's far-off screaming.

These are the badlands of your journey
Where no surface holds level, neither
Water nor earth can stay to its destiny.

Where light is what beats you down, out of
A massive sky. Your eyes, painfully
Hooded, encounter sheer, vertical faces.

Everywhere is laughter, social,
Mocking, the too-fast laughing of jackals,
Songs of self-justification.

Only one, a woman, a sender
Of quiet love-letters, eloquent
Of clean-cut Boston, testifies to mercy.

In far water, sliced by your dinghy
But closing at once behind, leaving
No memorial but the petrels' crying,

You had already known, at Cape Ann,
The vastness of God
                      and once, city
Streets melting into light, his silence.

Gradually you felt breeze on a scorched face,
Knew sails stirring.

In 1925 Eliot joined the new publishing house of Faber and Gwyer (shortly afterwards Faber and Faber), with which he was associated for the rest of his life.

'Journey of the Magi' (1927) was one of Eliot's first explicitly Christian poems.

In 1927 Eliot resumed his correspondence with Emily Hale, whom he had met in Boston possibly as early as 1908, and with whom he had been in love before the War. In all he wrote her over a thousand letters, all sequestered in the Library at Princeton until 2020. See Sections V-VI, and the second essay in this volume.

A LOVE AND ITS SOUNDING

Tight furled at the Bank.
Stiffly-reefed at Fabers', umbrellaed
Editor, literary lion, lost boy,

You write about a mage who somehow
Gets dispensation from his silken
Girls, from holidays connubial,

Write to long-remembered Emily,
Who lives far beyond desert, teaches
Sensibly in a college in Milwaukee.

You are afraid you will tell her you
Love her, cheating history, or worse
That she, redeeming time, may find you out,

Unpick the fabric, dissolve the dunes.
That she *does* love, and lets you know it,
And never claims you, this is grace indeed.

Grace beyond hope, for the logic
Of your few advisors
Is inexorable. In the waves of the desert

Dissolve hopes. There remain only
Forms of incantation
(God and Satan listening together)

Lord, now lettest... Now and in the hour
Of our deaths. Now that stone has been struck
For life's sake. For these eyes have seen

Flight and fire. Lord, now lettest.

The motif of the tempters comes from <u>Murder in the Cathedral</u> (1934).

A LOVE AND ITS SOUNDING

You attest to a God whose service
Is called, impossibly, in measured
English collects perfect freedom;

And at once, as though admitted by
The first inkling of the cadences
Of Cranmer, enter the fourfold tempters.

They process certainly the vast dark
Halls of your mind, are endured silent,
Knees ground into flagstones, not presuming.

The first – to recant into madness –
Easy enough to resist (for in
A dream, in which a flash-flood is hurtling

Down a steeply wooded valley, beech-
Green, dark-wrecked, torn by raging water,
A tree of life is clung to beyond strength),

The next two are the attendant lords
Of power and connivance. They are
Dressed like yourself in understatement,

In what can be understood in England
Between gentlemen and trustees. You hold
These in an anteroom, pay their stamp duties.

The last you know as well as your own
Life. He is not dismissed, because he
Cannot be. He perches, complacent, suave,

Cunning as a literary cat, atop
Your desk at Fabers', intrudes boldly
On your confessor's study, into prayer,

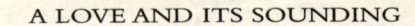

Vivien Eliot's mental health deteriorated steadily after the separation (see Section VI). Eliot remained one of the trustees of her estate.

Needs only the possibility
Of that old pride to gain admittance
To the exquisite realm of your suffering.

He is in your sense of self-regard;
He helps you with the chill blandishments
Of the first tempter. Not you, surely, Tom.

He advises, sweetly reasonable,
Understanding of your present dilemma,
In the difficult case of the other two:

What *is* required of the sane husband
Of hormones deemed mad? Where does prudence
End, and sheer abuse of power begin?

The soft voice suggests on, most of all
He gives power to your old power
To watch yourself, to watch yourself watching.

The agonized poet, hidden by
The Gioconda smile - that is what
He wants you to cultivate, idolise.

Or even better the Christian
Martyr, armed with powers of faith
And of forgetting self-inflicted chaos.

You set yourself strong in the structures
Of culture, decried them, then found that
Vast wilderness emptied their force,

Left your bones prey to a bleaching light,
To the blade-leaves of plants that flower
Once, if that, in the lifetime of a searcher.

A LOVE AND ITS SOUNDING

I want to say that you were saved
By things that endured from your childhood,
By the sweet thrush, and memory of the sea.

The truth is harsher; it tears at us –
Makes a claim – you were healed, fiercely, by
The twin eagles of love and repentance,

By whose eviscerating cries God
Was voiced, and darkness, and the salt river
Acknowledged, acerbically, run dry.

A LOVE AND ITS SOUNDING

V

They all appear jumbled together
In the record, faithfulness and doubt,
Mercy, betrayal, trust, transcendence.

Vital tracks are lost between stations –
Self-sabotaged. All that can be seen
Is exodus, eventual exile

(self-imposed) and between them the land
Of promise. Emily showed it you –
Believed that you could claim it. The Lord God

Made his claims too. The more you loved her
The more insistent divine demand,
No felicity escaping his gaze.

You could say of Christ that his truth
Had always awaited your return
Like the stream the leap of struggling salmon;

You might have said, but rarely did, that
Old friendship preceded disaster,
Stemmed from a time of integrity.

That it was therefore not wrong to walk
Mind stalled by wonder at Emily
(and every second later memorised),

To commit to letter the double-
Edged delight of contact. To progress
In verse around the spiral stair of healing

A reference to 'Burnt Norton' (1936), the opening of which was inspired by a walk taken by Eliot and Emily in the garden of a Gloucestershire manor-house in the summer of 1934. See Essay II of this volume.

A LOVE AND ITS SOUNDING

And into a yew-wood where this awed,
Unvoiced reverence could become the
Iconic, hardly tolerable vehicle

Of truths about God and wretched man.
Plain present possibility of there
Being a future licensed songs of time -

Beyond the wailing, double-stopped *fantasia*
Of your marriage, viola tones
Of Emily, wise love, memory of love.

You could admire her choice of envelope
And the bowl in which she kept apples
And write about the idly twittering world.

Her actual presence rare enough
In the elegant editor's life -
Guarded, only sketchily confided -

And the meetings themselves had a sketched
Quality - try as you might you couldn't
Extract their meaning, or master shyness.

Afterwards you could recollect just
Exactly the light, the blossom in
The lane, the tones of the hidden bird,

The very act of living was briefly
Its own delight - then the memory
Had again to be hidden, and lived from.

But through those meetings, constrained, proper,
Came a sense that you could speak as well
As pray, and be, at last, understood;

A LOVE AND ITS SOUNDING

That emotions could find their voices
As they do in the brave, exacting world
Of a Bach suite for harpsichord -

Every key, however remote,
The subject of singing, every
Dance gravely tried, brilliantly resolved.

(And how critical the choice of dance,
You so famous, alone, pursued by
So intense a sense of contamination.)

Emily, fine hair tied back, gaze calm,
Steady and unafraid, was at work
Like the restorer of some mediaeval folio -

A pagan lyric, ancient pages
Gummed together, poisoned by fear
At its most persistent. She sampled only with care -

Did not discuss your reputation
(which you said was already behind
You, fashioned out of pride and too much pain)

Or your part in suppressing a river,
Or your right to your menagerie
Of masks, each more distant than the last.

It was eminently possible
To debate Dryden, or yet Dante,
As a shell-crazed subaltern in a gas-hole

East of Ypres might speculate about
Birdsong, and thereby find common ground
With a stretcher-bearer, bridging chaos.

A LOVE AND ITS SOUNDING

A LOVE AND ITS SOUNDING

It came to be that you could stare at
Life again, as in childhood, discern,
Timeless within time, patterns of rosebuds.

It came to be your promised summer –
Brightness and idols – an arriving
Into – and knowing – your kingdom –

Within the turning territory
Of long-distance friendship at forty
The heart, the epitome of sweetness.

And with the brightest star, the morning,
It was sometimes given to you to be
Alone, separated only by spirit.

(This like, but yet not like, the one place
Of other intimate aloneness –
The peace where the Lord was pleased to dwell,

That place of knee-grinding penitence,
The flagstones of the confessional.)
But what the relation, what the will of God?

Emily the mirroring pool, friends
For support, rough flagstones for comfort.
The sacrament, meekly kneeling.

In June 1936 Vivien pretended to go to America to see Eliot's sister Marian, one of a number of stratagems she used to attract attention to her desertion by her husband. They had met only once after the separation, when she briefly confronted him at the Sunday Times Book Exhibition in 1935.

Maurice Haigh-Wood, Vivien's brother, wrote to Eliot in July 1938 to let him know that her doctor recommended she be certified insane. She was detained in Northumberland House, a private asylum in London.
John Hayward, a precocious young editor and critic disabled by muscular dystrophy, and Mary Trevelyan were close associates of Eliot's from the 'thirties until the time of the poet's second marriage. Hayward gave considerable help with the composition of <u>Four Quartets</u>; Mary twice proposed to Eliot after Vivien's death.
Virginia Woolf drowned herself in 1941.

VI

Vivien still pursues you, grimly,
Refusing unbelief in your love,
Stalking Fabers', turned aside by secretaries.

She fakes a trip to your family;
Emily's letters flow. Devotion
And desperation, both deceived in you.

Your *Vita Nuova* is lived in code,
By Emily's love, in fear of Viv
(until her family finally commit her),

While other friends, crippled young Hayward
And Mary Trevelyan, slide into
Your shy, aloof, catlike confidence.

Virginia, seeing you, the year
Before she killed herself, wrote of you
As wearing the great yellow bronze mask,

Your defences worn in on your self
As you went deeper, hoping to drown
In God, but well-versed mystic enough

To know that whatever did drown you
Would not, could not, be more than the
Dark that surrounds, and leaves us blind.

The bronze mask is for the day – the night
Sees pale silver light on your corroded
Face, coursed now by age's chasings.

The Family Reunion (1939) - see Essay II.

For example Archbishop Temple's Malvern Conference of 1941, and the working party on 'Catholicity' for Archbishop Fisher (1946-7).

'East Coker' (1940), 'The Dry Salvages' (1941), and 'Little Gidding' (1942).

A LOVE AND ITS SOUNDING

It is not direct moonlight. It is
Reflected in the face of a line
Of rocks jutting out to sea.

You have forsworn a plain moonsilver
And not even openly but through
A play about a man who cannot come home.

At one remove from facing love
You sit among the rocks, feel the sea
Swallow all light. You mark channels for others.

To be found with the rocks and the sky
Even that is not God, but feels not quite
So far from the shadow of the Crucified.

Your vigil among the terrible
Moiling waves is fed by friendship and
By what you take for body and blood –

With odd and stubborn conformity
Calling a Friday good. Calling prayer
Possible, serving on Anglican committees.

Behind blackout curtains, disciplined,
You write your three last songs, scriptural
In the solemnity of their speaking.

They look beyond your self for stillness.
You stare out towards the night
Towards a place where the Lord's song can be sung.

It is the last vision. To begin
Is to begin again, knowing yourself
Only as made, and made therefore only for God.

Eliot and Hayward moved into 19 Carlyle Mansions in early 1946, Eliot taking for his use the smaller rooms at the back of the flat.

Vivien Eliot, still in her sanatorium, died suddenly of heart failure on the night of January 22, 1947.

A reported recollection of Maurice Haigh-Wood's when close to his own death.

Henry Ware Eliot Jr. died in early May 1947.

A LOVE AND ITS SOUNDING

You set up house with Hayward, savour
All his caustic gossip, quick-witted,
And safely orbiting attentions of women.

These force-fields hold you in a space
Of safety, until the news comes that
Vivien has died, of a heart-attack.

She who had touched hyacinths, known you
Tiresias, Hieronymo, touched
All the women you would yearn to love,

Dead in her sanatorium, dead
Behind that nine-year-old instrument
Of committal, though her brother pronounced her

Shortly before, and with a certain
Puzzled and impotent bitterness,
As sane as he was himself, and left her there.

If publicly your bronze pose remains,
Sculptural, augmented by a slight
Extra frown, the private Furies return.

From the prayer of helpless grief you go
Quickly to the States, see your brother
Succumb to leukaemia. You plead now for time -

But the prophet of time is besieged
By honorary degrees, lectures
On the high call of poet. By Emily's wanting.

This new place, which under Canon Law
Is freedom, proves to be an exile
Self-mediated, discovered in the self

Deeper than deepest friendship,
Demanding distance. Now you are led
Far from the lotos, the high summer meadows,

Far from the love-court of the Temple.
Now you answer only the substance,
And not the heart, of Emily's letters.

Your life a land of bones, once breathed
Into song, glad to lie in a strange state
Sorrowing. A last expiation,

Beyond vigils. A last clouding of
Your spiritual sight, so you could be led
Blind back to Jerusalem.

A LOVE AND ITS SOUNDING

VII

I sit in the Church at East Coker
Your ashes' resting place. Above them
An understated epitaph –

You ask us from an oval tablet
To pray for the repose of the soul
Of Thomas Stearns Eliot, Poet.

There is a sense of our petitions
Being sought for yet longer struggle –
That the pale purgatorial fires

That beckoned you from the desert burn
Still. I do not believe it. The church,
The high dark Jacobean panelling,

The plain space of nave, checked floor, plain swept,
Sturdy house for the elusive God
Of earth and air, rose and fire, shelter

From our storm-flung present anarchy,
Speaks of stillness, clarity of light,
And of the Furies finally befriended.

What had been flight has become pure search.
What once penance, acceptance of blessing.
By what last charism, what alchemy?

I sit for a long time in the south aisle
Till the angle of the sun changes
And I see a single strand of spider's web.

Valerie Fletcher had aspired to be Eliot's secretary since reading 'Journey of the Magi' at the age of fourteen. She was appointed to the post in August 1950, by which time she was twenty-two. They fell in love, and married in January 1957, not quite ten years after Vivien's death. Eliot was then sixty-eight, and Valerie thirty. See Essay III.

The marriage, which was a total surprise to many of Eliot's closest friends, took place at 6.15a.m., not at St Stephen's, South Kensington, to which Eliot went on every other morning, but at St Barnabas', Addison Road. Stories vary as to when Hayward was given the news. It is clear that it was at a very late stage, and led to a major breach in the two men's friendship.

A LOVE AND ITS SOUNDING

The creature has spun it all the way
From window to dark oak chest, from light
To a locked, life-swallowing secret.

This filament, not easily seen
By aging eyes, but, once glimpsed, seeming
To carry all the light of that solemn place -

Not merely to dance with it, but to
Set it delightfully in balance,
Giving gravity its due, also love.

Thus, it seems, the gift of Valerie.

Under the strident adulation
A held cello-note, consistent, true,
Faithful to your every modulation.

A chord of homecoming, strength to spurn
Self-pity, the promise too of calm
Within the many clashes of weariness.

****

Thoughts of marrying invoked, of course,
The old conspiracies - stratagems
For avoiding Vivien, for staying free.

Secrets were second nature - the fear
Of ridicule, rebuff, intense at
Almost seventy. A profound embargo

Descended upon the news that you would,
After all, attempt happiness. Priests
Knew, your solicitor, eventually Hayward.

65

In 1948 Eliot was awarded both the Nobel Prize for Literature and the Order of Merit.

The marriage is the last known victory
Of joy, after badlands, the *Quartets*,
The honours heaped on you in Babylon.

The secrecy is a satisfaction
To the tempters. If perhaps it is
Your punishment that you never write

Great poetry again – it is accepted.
Now your eye sees God, in Valerie,
And no more needs to despise itself.

The walls of the new city are built
Out of straightforward gladness, the lie
To gossip given just by joy together.

Time present is the Beatles' England,
Profumo, the fourteenth Mr Wilson,
Technology's supposed white heat.

In America brilliant light falls
On the first killed Kennedy. Early
Advisors pack bags for Vietnam.

And Catholic tradition eases
Itself awake, a long-sleeping giant,
Moves on. In your last photographs

You always look cold, lean slightly on
Your wife, whose stubborn positive gaze
Sends out in clear the happiness you share.

What you write now is limpid, and lacks
Puritanical, mystical reach.
This is the high rock-pool of contentment

Eliot's last years contained much illness. He died on January 4, 1965.

A LOVE AND ITS SOUNDING

Where, under ominous skies, modern
Pollutions, botched genocides waiting
Their turn, you take shelter, rest.

****

One striving, among millions. I tell
Out those years; they are soon enough told.
But where hard meaning, beneath the history?

Perhaps that unconditional love,
Behind our rituals of meeting
And parting, is vanishingly rare

(bright and brief as sugar-maple fall,
Given inconveniently like
A hurried kiss, in a crowd, farewell,

Or endured for, in unknowing hope -
The occasional result of long
Patient sacrifice, which believes all things?)

That understanding, reaching beyond
The present, is only gathered in
When middle age slows the zesting pulse?

Or that all the finely-wrought cadences
In Christendom rate nothing without
The kindness that imagines the other's pain?

Your life is not so closed, or saintly,
As to condense easily into
Gospel, or eulogy, or cautionary tale.

A LOVE AND ITS SOUNDING

A LOVE AND ITS SOUNDING

The masterful voice of the four songs
Sounded your own hurt, used the torment
Of others, supposed all shattered anthems.

And every prayer found its mark
In mystery, difficult fusion
Of fire and fire, delight and death.

And every possibility not forbidden
Must be considered, and still the sum,
You want to say, is all composed of hope.

****

Who have I found? Not the sleek salmon
Or the practical cat - or - yes - both
Enciphered with the confidential clerk,

The curious boy and the terrified
Lover, tight-furled editor, mystic,
The long accepter of longer penance.

Above all an old, sad soul from the age
Of Titans, and a Christian who died
In his bed, with a wife to comfort him.

For which last mercy
May thanks be.

A LOVE AND ITS SOUNDING

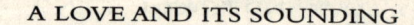

Three Essays on Eliot

I. Bleistein derided: Eliot and anti-Semitism

II. That she *does* love: Eliot and Emily

III. Calling a Friday good: Eliot and faith

A LOVE AND ITS SOUNDING

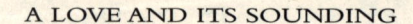

Essay I: Bleistein derided - Eliot and anti-Semitism

No treatment of Eliot's life as a whole can now omit mention of the anti-Semitism evident in some of his early poems, in prose written after his conversion, and in various letters and personal contacts.

This concern is altogether appropriate, but surprisingly recent. The subject was raised by Christopher Ricks in his *T.S.Eliot and Prejudice*[1], but in a way which largely exculpated the poet. Before that it had had periodic but glancing critical attention. But with Anthony Julius' vigorous and comprehensive condemnation in *T.S.Eliot, anti-Semitism and literary form*[2], and the very public disagreements his book has evoked, this perspective on Eliot becomes inescapable.

Before the present controversy it was at least possible for someone who, like myself, loved *Four Quartets*, could only admire *The Waste Land*, and thoroughly disliked the *Ara Vos Prec* poems, to skate over the latter in forming an overall sense of Eliot. Indeed Lyndall Gordon does precisely this in the best biographical studies to date[3]. Gordon has shed most helpful light on *The Waste Land* as religious poem, and on Emily Hale, but because of these emphases Gordon's concern is very much with the early Eliot's spiritual reading, and with 'La Figlia...', rather than with 'Burbank...', or yet 'Dirge'.

Julius' book, and its review by Louis Menand[4], reject such partial lighting of the drama of Eliot's life. Menand shows how much of the legacy of Eliot's time in Paris was not merely aesthetic but political, philosophical and anti-Semitic, in particular from his contacts with Charles Maurras and the *Action Française*. Julius catalogues subsequent anti-Semitic work, including: 'Gerontion', 'Burbank with a Baedeker: Bleistein with a Cigar', 'Sweeney Among the Nightingales', 'A Cooking Egg', the particularly abominable 'Dirge' (a suppressed draft for *The Waste Land*[5]), *Sweeney Agonistes*, and certain prose pieces, especially Eliot's first Page-Barbour Lecture at the University of Virginia in 1933 - published in *After Strange Gods*[6].

1. London: Faber & Faber, 1988.
2. Cambridge: CUP, 1995.
3. *Eliot's Early Years* (Oxford: OUP, 1977) and *Eliot's New Life* (Oxford: OUP, 1988).
4. In *The New York Review of Books*, *43*, 10, pp34-41 (1996).
5. 'Dirge' can be found in *The Waste Land: a facsimile and transcript* ed.Valerie Eliot (London: Faber & Faber, 1971) pp119-21.
6. London: Faber & Faber; New York: Harcourt, Brace, 1934.

I agree with Julius as to his assessment of Part IV of *The Waste Land*: that what remains in this section is purified of the grotesque and bitter spirit of 'Dirge'. (Indeed it shows that universalising of experience, transcending prejudice, which is found in the very best of the Christian inspiration, e.g. at Galatians 3.28[7].) I accept however that a body of poems written before 1920, and certain other pieces, particularly a published lecture of 1933, show clear evidence of anti-Jewish prejudice[8].

I pass to the arguments deployed about the material. Julius' most telling point is that Eliot was 'that rarest type of anti-Semite – one who put his prejudice at the service of his art'. In this he echoes and develops a remark of George Steiner's made many years ago – that 'Eliot's uglier touches tend to occur at the heart of very good poetry'[9]. This is a vital point. If the relevant poems are seen as minor, then, as James Wood observed in reviewing Julius[10], 'so is Eliot's anti-Semitism' (at least in literary, if not in spiritual terms). Julius' argument is directly to the contrary – it is that the anti-Semitism is in the art, <u>and</u> *that it is what helps to make the poetry as fine as it is*. As Menand paraphrases, 'there is no artistic difference between Bleistein and the hyacinth girl'.

I find this charge proven only in the case of 'Burbank'. I place the other poems listed above in a different category. The anti-Semitic passage in 'Gerontion', though characteristically cleverly sounded, is not central to the poem's thesis, nor does it further it. Wood again: "'Gerontion' is a poem with an anti-Semitic rash, but the rash is confined to a limb"[11]. Much the same could be said of *Sweeney Agonistes*.

The 'Rachel née Rabinovich' reference in 'Sweeney Among the Nightingales', although cited by Steiner, seems to me crude and clotted; if it is in proximity to 'very good poetry', it forms no essential part of it. And it is dubious if 'A Cooking Egg' is more than minor.

'Dirge' belongs in a category of its own. If a student had brought me such a piece I would have thought it evidence more than anything else of mental illness. It is an again clever but crazed meditation on corporeal decay; if anything warranted Eliot's own expectation of the reception of his work of

---

7. Written by a writer with whom Eliot shows some parallels, Paul of Tarsus – see Essay III.
8. To Julius' list can be added a few letters – Peter Ackroyd in his *T.S. Eliot* (London: Hamish Hamilton, 1984) lists four: that to Pound on 31.10.17, to Quinn on 12.3.23, to Read on 16.2.25(?), and to Dobrée around March 1929.
9. *The Listener*, 29.4.71.
10. In *New Republic*, 29.7.96.
11. I reject as fanciful Julius' derivation of the opening 'Here I am' from Yahweh's self-revelation in Exodus – it surely belongs with the languor of Prufrock's 'Let us go' and the world-weariness of the tone of 'Gerontion' as a whole.

this period 'in America I shall be thought merely disgusting'[12] it would have been 'Dirge'. Fortunately Eliot, going beyond Pound's mere scrawl 'Doubtful' on the fair copy, suppressed it. [Though it is disconcerting that, unlike the crude and obscene Bolo poems (recently published in *Inventions of the March Hare*[13]), he *did* consider using it in work for publication.] Even Craig Raine's valiant effort to declare the charge of anti-Semitism unproven falters at 'Dirge', which he records as 'dangerously co-terminous with anti-Semitism'[14].

Only in the poem 'Burbank with a Baedeker: Bleistein with a Cigar' is Julius' major point well made. Only here does the sordid theme actually 'work' artistically, as it does in that *locus classicus* of anti-Semitism, *The Merchant of Venice*. Not coincidentally 'Burbank' is an evocation of Venice, albeit a 'dissolving' one[15]. Here Eliot's Jamesian play of character across the 'narrative' makes use of caricature of Jewishness in an exquisitely clever way, in particular at that moment when a new stanza commutes the grand 'Sir Ferdinand' (to whom the Princess Volupine goes from the naïve Burbank) with the single word 'Klein'. This is a poetic joke almost worthy of the Rabbinic tradition itself, deployed here in what Eliot himself called an 'intensely serious' poem, and 'among the best I have ever done'[16].

So in 'Burbank' Eliot the young ironist in the enervating marriage, estranged from his family, still mourning a father who had rejected Vivien to the last – even cutting her out of his will – Eliot who had read most things and had no secure grip on anything, did 'achieve' an anti-Semitic work of art. [Even Raine, the most determined of Eliot's current defenders (the more remarkable since Raine is himself Jewish), concedes that 'Burbank' is 'a difficult poem to defend'[17].] And it forever must be held against Eliot's artistic judgment that such ingenuity was deployed to serve such prejudice, and that he retained work of this kind in all his subsequent collections.

---

12. Letter to Henry Ware Eliot Jr, 15.2.20, [*The Letters of T.S.Eliot, Vol. 1, 1898-1922*, ed. Valerie Eliot (London: Faber & Faber, 1988), p363].
13. Edited by Christopher Ricks (London: Faber & Faber, 1996).
14. *Financial Times*, 18.5.96. 'Weasel words' (Julius, *Observer* 15.9.96) indeed. The last fragment in *The Waste Land Facsimile* (p123) shows a much more tender use of the Ariel song, Eliot possibly recalling the dead Jean Verdenal.
15. The term is Piers Gray's, from *T.S.Eliot's Intellectual and Poetic Development 1909-22* (Brighton: Harvester Press, 1982).
16. In the letter to Henry Eliot quoted above. Wood has underrated 'Burbank' in thinking of it as verse powered by 'the smaller category of sarcasm'.
17. Despite his strange reading of the 'lustreless protrusive eye' as a description of a sunset.

Even more damaging to Eliot's reputation as a Christian artist must be his remark in the Virginia lectures of 1933 about the undesirability of having many 'free-thinking Jews' in a Christian society. Eliot was by then in middle life, a prince of letters, a critic without peer, a publicly-professed Christian. It is not enough that the lectures were not republished after their first printing. It is not enough that this was a time when fears of Jewish influences on capitalism were strongly and widely expressed, as were other political opinions now easily seen to be bankrupt. Nor is it enough that this was the American visit by dint of which Tom finally left Vivien, a time therefore of great personal turmoil.

Raine makes a valiant effort to moderate what seems now like the total crassness of this remark. His point that Eliot is not advocating an absolute intolerance is well made. But at the very least Eliot shows a marked insensitivity to the way the world was developing in the 1930s.

This insensitivity is seen in even sharper focus when it is noted that Eliot, for a public reading at the Wigmore Hall in September 1943, chose 'Gerontion' as one of his two selections from the whole of his work. 'the jew squats', read, as Julius points out, in the year of the destruction of the Warsaw Ghetto.

To what can we ascribe this? There is, perhaps, a hint at least in the phrase from the end of 'A Love and its Sounding', 'an old sad soul from the age of Titans'. Eliot was a conservative born in the 19th Century. For all his aesthetic innovations, which still challenge the poet of today, and the profundity of his later spiritual life, his political and social instincts developed before the First World War. His views on the dynamics of society were formed in a Maurrassian, anti-Dreyfusard crucible already reactionary in 1912. He seems altogether to have failed to grasp the character of the abomination that was growing at the heart of Christendom as the 'thirties unfolded, and first books, and then humans, were destroyed without ceremony[18].

Were the charge of anti-Semitism proven, Raine alleges that 'it would effectively occlude the literary achievement'. He is the one of the few still able to regard the charge as unproven, but there is no sign (bar the odd captious and slight reviewer[19]) that Eliot's standing as a poet is in jeopardy. Rather TSE's work has to be evaluated from a different spiritual standpoint; 'Journey of the Magi', 'Ash Wednesday', and *Four Quartets* are not the work of a saint,

18. His incomprehension of the all-encompassing evil of Nazism seems to have persisted into the period of the War itself – in a letter to Betjeman on 18.9.39 he recommends men to be preserved for important post-war work *independent of the result of that war* [quoted in John X. Cooper's *T.S. Eliot and the Ideology of <u>Four Quartets</u>* (Cambridge: CUP, 1995) p112].
19. Such as Bevis Hillier in *The Spectator*, 7.9.96.

but of a believer with many blind-spots, a man conscious of many 'things ill done'[20], a man who continued to struggle and blunder in his intractable personal life (as in his assessment of his early poems, and, as Julius shows, in his reaction to critics of those poems[21]) to the end of his days.

So we see in Eliot both a degree of prejudice and a marked myopia as to its possible effects. The origins of such attitudes were no doubt complex. Julius notes three chemistries of anti-Semitism which may have combined in Eliot – that of America (both 'nativist' and 'élite'), that of French reactionary intellectuals, and that of the English literary tradition, stemming back to such seminal works as *The Merchant of Venice* and *The Jew of Malta*.

One important element in this may have been his Southernness. Julius quotes W.J.Cash: 'the Jew, with his eternal refusal to be assimilated, is everywhere the eternal Alien, and in the South, where any difference had always stood out with great vividness, he was especially so'[22]. Empson remarks that 'the young Eliot had a good deal of simple old St Louis brashness' [such a man would think the English policy 'towards the lower races dangerously permissive'][23]. At Harvard he rapidly shed his Southern accent; he assimilated himself into the intellectual society of the time. We know from his poems that he did not do so without ironic self-examination. But the assimilation did not abolish his (largely unexamined) Southern background. Even today a prejudice survives that Southerners living in the North are a slow, unsophisticated minority. In Eliot's anxiety to be part of the 'in' group he may have projected some of his resentment at this attitude into an accepted target for prejudice, a minority often regarded as *over*-sophisticated. And if in Boston Eliot felt himself, for all the impeccable nature of his connections, to have come from the wrong place, how much more so may this have been true in England. There he mixed with a set accustomed to privilege and to the supposed superiority of everything English, and largely possessed of secure private incomes (something which after his marriage his family denied him).

20. Not that I can agree with Ricks that this phrase in 'Little Gidding' refers to Eliot's regretting of anti-Jewish sentiments. Not even a far more strident anti-Semite than Eliot would characterise these, in a poem of the precision and high spiritual tone of *Four Quartets*, as things that had once been taken 'for exercise of virtue'.
21. There is a baffling ingenuousness in Eliot's letter to the *TLS* of 23.8.57 asking on what grounds he is charged with anti-Semitism, and the query is very properly swept away by Christopher Logue's reply in the same journal of September 6. Eliot's ensuing silence is in stark contrast to his vigorous legal action against John Peter's article in *Essays in Criticism*, 2, 3, pp242-66 (1952) alleging homosexual attachment in his friendship with Verdenal.
22. Julius, ..*anti-Semitism*.., p158.
23. In *Using Biography* (London: Chatto & Windus, 1984), pp189-200.

So insofar as his anti-Semitism exceeded that which was normally expressed within his cultural and social group I suggest that we may find this associated with (though not justified by) his desire to move into acceptability and respectability within the ruling culture[24].

Empson has a most interesting theory as to the unconscious drive behind the anti-Semitism of *Ara Vos Prec* and *The Waste Land* drafts, namely that this stemmed from the projection of rage at his father, a 'purse-proud' Unitarian who felt his son had failed him, and who even in his will disowned that wayward son's marriage. This certainly fits with the crazed intensity of 'Dirge' - again it is the dispassionate artistry of 'Burbank' which is harder to swallow[25].

Anthony Julius has overstated his case, but, like the advocate he is, he has made a big impact on the jury. Craig Raine is valiant but wrong, both in his refusal to accept the charge of anti-Semitism against Eliot and in his assessment of the consequences of the charge's being proven. The spiritual achievement of the life *is* diminished by Eliot's failure to address the offence of the anti-Semitisms. The constellation of his literary achievement is seen to contain some less flattering stars than were previously evident, but not by any means occluded.

****

In the context of this debate it may seem odd, particularly to Jewish readers, to be publishing a poem in which the motifs of the Hebrew Bible are used to describe Eliot's own life. No element of irony - still less a desire to offend - formed any part of the original framing of the poem or contributes to its publication at this juncture. Rather the architecture of the poem reflects a conviction as to the universality of the biblical motifs - they reflect the dealings of God with human beings and hence, or so the Jewish or Christian believer will hold, the most fundamental dynamic of human life.

---

24. So Frederic Raphael: Eliot was 'in many ways, a conventional man, hot for homogeneity, and ... like many metics - he ran for cover by running with the hounds' (*TLS* 19.7.96).
25. Perhaps we see in 'Burbank' a very conscious use of the objective correlative (for helpless ennui at the decay of European society) which Eliot described, once and once only and at the same period, in his famous essay on *Hamlet* (*Selected Essays*, London: Faber & Faber, 3rd edn, 1951, p141f). If so, it is no surprise that he found part of the thought-form of the poem in another Shakespearean trope, the reviling of Shylock.

Essay II - That she *does* love: Eliot and Emily

At the beginning of a recent essay Bernard Sharratt offers a bare outline of a view now very commonly accepted in Eliot studies:
> Eliot was in love with Emily Hale. He married Vivien Haigh Wood. The marriage was an appalling disaster....In 1934 and 1935 Emily was in England. Eliot and Emily visit Burnt Norton. From that comes *Burnt Norton* (what might have been).....[1]

This view has developed out of Lyndall Gordon's painstaking and sympathetic research on this relationship. She records Eliot receiving a letter from a long-lost Boston friend, presumably the start of the famous correspondence of which Emily's letters are (presumably) destroyed, and Eliot's to her are locked away in Princeton Library until 2020[2].

One of the few dissenting voices is that of Mrs Valerie Eliot, who, in a rare interview given to Blake Morrison, alleged that a friend of Emily's had made a point of telling her that 'this theory of Tom's great love for [Emily] was all rubbish'[3].

This is a thin protest, relying on an unnamed source. The protest is anyway unnecessary. There is not a shred of evidence that the long friendship was at any point sexual, or that it persisted into the time of Eliot's intimacy with his second wife. Mrs Eliot herself admits in her Biographical Commentary to her edition of Eliot's Letters that the young Eliot did fall in love with Emily[4]. Lyndall Gordon's reconstruction of the subsequent dynamic of the relationship is eminently plausible, and has formed the basis for the heart of my poem.

I have, then, rejected the caution of Moody who in the preface to his 1994 edition of *Thomas Stearns Eliot Poet*[5] states that he continues to omit

1. In his 'Modernism, Postmodernism, and After' in *The Cambridge Companion to T.S.Eliot*, ed. A.David Moody (Cambridge: CUP, 1994).
2. As well as the fact of the letters, an important element in the evidence on Emily is a series of gifts made to her by Eliot. Gordon records in particular his sending of his essay 'Shakespeare and the Stoicism of Seneca' in 1927, with its mention of a poet's dependence on his own emotions and memories. In her essay in *Words in Time* (ed. E.Lobb, London: The Athlone Press, 1993, pp38-51) she mentions an earlier gift, of *Ara Vos Prec* in 1923 (why that book? and why then?) with an emotive inscription from Eliot's beloved Dante.
3. *The Independent on Sunday*, 24.4.94.
4. *The Letters of T.S.Eliot, Volume I, 1898-1922*, ed. V. Eliot (London: Faber & Faber, 1988), xxi.
5. 2nd edition, with a new introduction, Cambridge: CUP, 1994.

Emily from his critical study of Eliot because 'we are simply not in possession of the relevant information'. If the thousand letters that will be available in 2020 had been destroyed, literary biography would not have hesitated to draw conclusions about Emily's effects on Eliot. That the next generation of scholars will have the letters does not mean that this one cannot benefit from other inferences, admittedly provisional[6].

The difficulty in evaluating this friendship lies not only in the embargo on the principal remaining source material. At this early stage it is too easy to take sides – to reconstruct Vivien as a Zelda Fitzgerald figure as in the (gravely misleading) film *Tom and Viv*, to espouse the cause of Emily as Lyndall Gordon does (however sensitively) in *Eliot's New Life*, or to defend the great man's memory as Valerie Eliot does so resolutely.

My focus here is Eliot himself. In his drama and in *Four Quartets* we continually see how beneath the surface of everyday life he conceives a world of moral inexorability (evinced in particular by the Eumenides of *The Family Reunion*) and of spiritual necessities (the 'prayer, observance, discipline, thought and action' of 'The Dry Salvages' V). It is my belief that Eliot could endure his contact with this moral world, of which he felt so unworthy (feeling as he did so keenly the consequences of his first marriage and his failure to live it through), only through two factors. These at first operated together:

Firstly, he discovered the apparatus of Christian, particularly Anglo-Catholic, spirituality, with its sacramental rhythm in which confession and absolution led up to the eucharist.

Secondly, he discovered in Emily, or perhaps more accurately in the mixture of bright adolescent love and mature personal esteem that thinking of her evoked, affirmation of himself as a person.

The term 'sounding' in my title has two senses. Firstly, that love for Emily sounds through much of Eliot's verse, in particular the woman imagined weeping after the parting of lovers in 'La Figlia Che Piange', the lady of the 'turning brown hair' in 'Ash Wednesday', the companion at the never-quite-entered rose-garden in 'Burnt Norton', and the two central women in *The Family Reunion*. Secondly, that the depths of this still-little-understood love remain obscure. All the critic can do, in verse or prose, is test for echoes, try to establish how many fathoms the friendship between Eliot and Emily extended below the surface of their lives.

6. Moody breaks his own stricture in a recently published essay – 'Being in fear of women' in his *Tracing T.S.Eliot's Spirit* (Cambridge: CUP, 1996, pp182-95), in which he makes a number of telling observations precisely on the relation of Emily to Eliot's verse, especially *The Family Reunion*.

In the centre of my poem I explore this, and poetry is the better medium for the exploration[7]. It can make most eloquent use of the bare account available to us while the thousand letters are still sequestered[8]. But in this essay I draw out further some of the strands the poem explores.

We can say, without those letters, that Eliot's belief in himself, which when he was a young man was always erratic, took savage punishment from the failure of his marriage to Vivien. What Emily Hale gave him, out of love and friendship and the hope that they might one day be together, was precisely, ironically enough, her success at managing the single life – her ability to walk alone into a room, her beautiful brown hair tied back and her head held high, seeking whatever zest literature and culture and society might offer. The letters quoted by Gordon from after the cooling of the friendship in the 'fifties show the extent to which this sense of self was a casualty of their unconsummated love.

Eliot was influenced towards developing a religious allegiance by Charles Maurras. It is also known that he was much swayed by two other spiritual searchers, Paul Elmer More and William Force Stead[9]. Male figures, as of course were the priests with whom his new commitment brought him into contact. Given the extent to which Eliot was influenced throughout his life by women it is not surprising that the matrix of influences on his 'new life' also contained a profoundly significant female figure. Emily's attitude to Eliot's conversion is one of the many questions about which we are unlikely to know more until the release of the letters in 2020. A related question is to what extent the Emily of 1927-39 represented for Eliot principally the unconditionally admiring figure his mother had once been, or the 'wise woman' depicted in Agatha in *The Family Reunion*, or a symbol of innocence, of the single life untouched by the sexual miasma into which the poet of 'Ode' and 'Sweeney Among the Nightingales' felt himself to have fallen.

7. 'What logical thought cannot say, poetry can, but in such a way that the reader has to play his part.' (V.A.Demant at Eliot's Requiem Mass, St Stephen's, South Kensington, 17.2.65).
8. Even the correspondence may not be conclusive; I think we shall find the long-awaited letters predominantly literary in content, with a constant theme of Eliot's gratitude for Emily's friendship and attentiveness. I suspect they will appear formal, almost 19th-Century in tone, lacking the sharp mockery we see for instance in his letters to Pound, or yet the playfulness of his 'Cat' conceits.
9. For Eliot's admiration for More see A.H.Dakin's *Paul Elmer More* (Princeton: Princeton U.P., 1960) – also TSE's tribute to More quoted in Essay III. Stead has a wonderful little passage in his *The Shadow of Mount Carmel* (London: R.Cobden-Sanderson, 1926) about a type of writer with 'Studied Cruelty of Outlook' (pp38-9) which might be aimed directly at the Eliot of *Ara Vos Prec*.

From the late 1920s on, Eliot drew energy, of various kinds, from this precious friendship, and he drew forgiveness from his religious observance (see Essay III). In 1933 he finally left his wife, counter to the spirit of the teachings of the Lord to whom he had publicly given allegiance. The sense of conflict attached to this decision must have been intense. It is worked out, at least to some extent, in *The Family Reunion*. Here Eliot uses a hero who has come back 'home' without his wife, for whose death he may or may not have been responsible. But strikingly the playwright does not cast Harry's moral quandaries in Christian terms – that would have been unbearable – but in the framework of Greek tragedy[10]. Moreover the alternative female figure is split – my contention is that *both* 'Agatha' and 'Mary' represent facets of Emily Hale[11].

Harry's predicament in *The Family Reunion* is vigorously drawn, but it is a dilution of Eliot's own moral predicament – irrevocably committed to the Christian Church, passionately in love with and emotionally dependent upon a woman other than his wife, unable any longer to face that wife's illness (in respect of which, it must be remembered, male-dominated medical science had only very limited understanding and sympathy[12]).

Perhaps only saints resolve predicaments of this severity. Eliot's own response is a much more familiar one: he piloted his way through the situation, avoiding the terrible whirlpools represented by the need to return to Vivien, or again the possibility of having to do without Emily. Both of these options represented for him the certainty of emotional collapse (with the symptoms of which he was already familiar from the early 1920s).

---

10. Even at the time it was noticed that this diluted the power of the play. See Desmond McCarthy's review in *The New Statesman and Nation*, 25.3.39.

11. 'Mary' no doubt contains elements of how Eliot *remembered* Emily from before the First World War. But a letter to Martin Browne about the play, part of which is in the Hayward Papers, implies that 'Mary' is not *merely* a remembered attraction, but an old attraction seen in a new light in a new situation. Emily *did* offer the 'spring and sunlight' associated in the play with Mary. But she was also an acute and devoted student of Eliot's work. She gave, I suggest, the sort of advice and guidance he might have received from a much older friend. Her life was an example of dedication within the field in which she found herself. Exemplary of '*agatha*' – good things, in the world of Greek tragedy on which the play draws so heavily. It is through his great scene with *Agatha* that Harry discovers his destiny.

12. Not that it was only men who failed to sympathise; Virginia Woolf produces some unforgettably scornful phrases for Vivien, of which 'the ether, the whistle, the dog' particularly sticks in the memory [letter to Ottoline Morrell, 22.6.32, published in *The Letters of Virginia Woolf*, ed. N.Nicolson & J.Trautmann, Vol. 5 (London: Hogarth Pr., 1979)]. The physiological effect of Vivien's practice of continually bathing her skin with diethyl ether could only have been profoundly damaging.

A LOVE AND ITS SOUNDING

So Eliot (presumably) both confessed and enjoyed his extramarital love[13], the luxury of heart and mind represented by contact with a spirit which seemed so to understand and resonate with his own. He gave Emily an elk-hound. They walked together at Burnt Norton, in New Hampshire, in California. She battled for a greater role for Mary in *The Family Reunion*. He drew from their renewed but unconsummable felicity the energy for great poetry - poetry of longing, renunciation, acceptance, Christian hope. *Four Quartets* was a sequence begun when their friendship was at its height, a sequence brought to fulfilment only once the war had imposed a distance which proved (for him) profoundly creative.

Although Eliot was a man of many calculations (as his correspondence reveals), I do not for a moment accuse him of having calculated this course of action. I suggest that the piloting was largely instinctive, motivated by love, fear, and fiercely-clung-to religious observance.

That the compromise between his Christian faith, his love for Emily, and his sense of moral obligation was ultimately a bankrupt one was shown by his reaction to the news of Vivien's death[14]. The accumulated guilt of twenty years' compromise burst upon him with terrible force. If the usual story is to be believed it was one of the few moments when his 'mask' cracked totally.

Richard Shusterman suggests that what Eliot sought after his conversion was the old Aristotelian virtue of *phronesis*, a wisdom which 'extends beyond proper thought and action to include proper feelings as well, which can likewise be trained, and which are needed to ensure that proper action be done without incurring painful internal conflict'[15]. On the scheme I am proposing here the internal conflicts remained sharp, but Emily's friendship gave Eliot the psychic energy, the joy at being alive, partly to bury the conflict, partly to transmute it into poetry.

Much had been shared with Emily: the processes of Eliot's art, his ceaseless reflection on the literary traditions that had shaped him, the many landscapes they had walked through on their vacations together. But she seems (if we follow Gordon here) to have misjudged totally his reaction to his wife's

---

13. Though reading the letters to Stead kept at Yale has made me wonder if Eliot ever told any *one* of his advisors about every aspect of his relationships. Stead arranged Eliot's baptism and confirmation, and seems to have been at times a valued confidant. There are definite hints that he knew something of the friendship with Emily, but he never met Vivien.
14. There are differing accounts: the generally accepted one is retold by Ackroyd (*T.S. Eliot*, p284). The overall effect seems to have been one of emotional and spiritual devastation.
15. Shusterman, 'Eliot as Philosopher' in *The Cambridge Companion...* pp31-47.

death – that it would not liberate him to express finally his love for her, but drive him deeper into celibacy and penance. That his struggle for *phronesis* would then finally enter its mature phase.

Emily wrote to Lorraine Havens[16]: 'he loves me – I believe that wholly – but apparently not in the way usual to men less gifted i.e. with complete love thro' a married relationship'. In another letter, quoted by Cynthia Ozick[17], she wrote to Princeton: '(The) man I loved, *I* think, did not respond as he should have to my long trust, friendship and love'. After his marriage to Valerie, Emily Hale made largely abortive, or ignored, efforts to register the relationship in other ways, by preserving both sides of their correspondence, by giving Eliot's gifts of his books to various libraries, by offering readings of his poetry. All this makes tragically clear how much of 'the cleft Eliot', the inner compromise within the poet, was hidden from Emily. Had she seen more clearly into it she might have realised much earlier that in the matrix of Eliot's faith, love, and art she would eventually be the loser[18]. She would have had the chance to bear that reality while her energy and courage were still with her.

Eliot consciously or unconsciously denied her that insight. The result was that he wrote a final burst of great poetry, the last three *Quartets*, but he prevented their relationship, which his letters to her may show to have been one of the most remarkable friendships in the history of modern literature, from reaching its full richness.

Could anything have made it different? One suspects not. No amount of Emily's presence could have been decisive while Vivien lived, and when she died Eliot had already, as Gordon points out, 'seen himself as a middle-aged man'[19], to whom only a state of non-attachment was appropriate.

There is in the Hayward Papers a photograph of special poignancy towards the end of a small photograph album of Vivien's dated 1924-9. These dates suggest that this particular shot may have been taken in '28 or '29.

'T.S.E.' is standing in the garden of Chester Terrace in an unusually expansive stance, open-toed, smiling, an open-hearted slightly gangling Missourian of (say) forty, a man at last coming to terms with himself.

---

16. 7.8.47, reproduced in Gordon, *Eliot's New Life*, pp170-1.
17. In her article, 'A Critic At Large', *The New Yorker*, 20.11.89, pp119-54.
18. As Moody comments ('*Tracing...*' p191), she must have allowed herself to be blind to what was implicit in *The Family Reunion*. She must also have failed to follow the spiritual movement of *Four Quartets* towards the renunciation of desire, its quenching in the fire of the Spirit.
19. *The Cocktail Party*, Act 1, Scene 2.

Could it be that on this particular day it seemed to him that his faith had at last fallen into place, that the intimate, life-giving friendship which brought memories of happiness into focus was once again in flower, and that, just possibly, his marriage might still be salvageable? If so it is particularly sad to reflect that it was not for almost thirty years that the combination of faith-commitment, sweet and intimate female friendship, and rewarding marriage finally came to him[20].

In my first essay I mentioned the legacy of Eliot's Southern upbringing. I believe this may also be seen in these awkward severings of close personal ties. Southern kindness can run very deep. But the social idiom of the well-to-do white South tends to be one of great surface charm which can be persisted with despite extraordinary personal animosities. When the surface gives way it may do so with great violence (as William Faulkner and Flannery O'Connor both so memorably chronicled). A feud may move from being utterly unspoken to a complete separation within a very short time. Eliot effected a number of major separations for very different motives: utter exhaustion of his charity and patience with Vivien; fear, with Emily, of an intimacy he could not reconcile with his guilt; in the case of John Hayward and Mary Trevelyan his desperate need to protect his improbable last romance. But the pattern of exclusion — the surface maintained until the last possible moment, the hurt effected without the feelings ever being disclosed — that I suggest may well have been a pattern learned in his Southern childhood.

Eliot formed for himself a quite magisterial position in the literary establishment of the English-speaking world, and he also became a spokesman for the Christian Church. The authoritative, numinous voice of the later Eliot, which developed through the thirties and culminates in the achievement of *Four Quartets*, is at its finest when it crystallises, however obliquely, a deep truth about the human individual's relation to time, to history, to the future. It is at its worst when, with seemingly equal authority, it excludes an individual or a group, as in the disastrous remark about 'free-thinking Jews' in the Virginia lectures.

'And in his public utterance, so in his (very) private life. He was proverbial in his circle in later life for his great personal kindness, for the trouble he took over young writers, the wit and sense of fun in Old Possum and his practical jokes at Fabers. And yet at the junctures when he deemed it

---

20. The significance of the otherwise disappointing late poem 'A Dedication to My Wife' lies in the bequeathing 'in public' of the 'rose-garden' to Valerie, a statement that in her alone did he now find 'leaping delight'.

necessary to exclude someone from the inner circle of his life this was done with formality combined with evasiveness tantamount to cruelty. Most evidently in disposing of Vivien by solicitor's letter. Almost as alarmingly in his sudden dispensing with Hayward's friendship on the occasion of his second marriage[21]. The manner of the change in his friendship with Emily Hale is not yet known to us: was it brought about with sympathy (even if she could not understand it), or was this the greatest, the most expedient unkindness of all?

---

21. Again, accounts differ as to how much warning Hayward had that the friend with whom he had lived for so long was deserting him. What is clear is that the friendship never recovered. In 1936 Eliot had removed the original dedication 'To My Wife' from 'Ash Wednesday'. In 1960 Faber issued the exquisite Mardersteig-printed limited edition of the *Quartets*. Eliot allowed this to omit the particular acknowledgement of Hayward's contribution that earlier editions had carried. The omission continued in the 1963 edition of the *Collected Poems*.

Essay III: Calling a Friday good - Eliot and faith

The starting point for this essay is Jody Bottum's 1995 article[1] in which he makes the startling and deliberately provocative assertion that T.S.Eliot never believed in God. States of belief are of course extraordinarily difficult to establish, but in this essay I take issue with Bottum through his subsidiary point that the work of Eliot's that shows his closest approach to faith is 'Ash Wednesday'. The spirituality of *Four Quartets* he finds 'merely weak and strange'. Bottum has altogether failed to discern the profound and deeply Christian movement of the poetry from 'Burnt Norton' to 'Little Gidding'[2].

The spiritual dynamic of the first few years after Eliot's conversion, the time of 'Ash Wednesday', was mainly about the possibility of addressing the enormous guilt he felt over his marriage. Faith meant access to the spiritual disciplines of confession, absolution and the eucharist, and to the stern counsel of the priests to whom he entrusted himself. To judge from Virginia Woolf's intermittent but always perceptive comments on him, he knew the *joy* of the Christian believer only after his advisors sanctioned his separation from Vivien, leaving him free 'to live, to love' (Virginia's phrase)[3].

Over the next few years he tasted both the happiness and the ambiguity of his intense friendship with Emily Hale. He had found someone who responded to him unconditionally, and who would receive whatever of himself he chose to disclose, but whom he could not marry. 'Burnt Norton', a poem placed in the garden in which they walked together in 1934, a poem among other things about tentative grasp for meaning, and whatever 'might have been', bears two epigraphs from Heraclitus. Indeed it is a Heraclitean meditation on the flow of time, stemming from that unrecapturable, unforgettable experience with Emily, as much as a Christian poem. (When 'the Word' finally appears in Section V it is fugitive, attacked by temptation, by a 'disconsolate chimaera', is only barely the Christian Logos rather than that of Heraclitus.) The immensely poignant conclusion to the poem is that there is a realm of timeless beauty, but our every attempt to reach it is marked by inadequacies, by the 'ridiculous' 'waste sad time' of the coda.

1. In *First Things*, August/September (1995), pp25-30.
2. Significantly Bottum calls the passage of 'Little Gidding' ending 'History is now and England' the 'conclusion' of the poem. 'Little Gidding' runs for 22 further lines, and its conclusion is far finer and further-reaching than Bottum allows.
3. *The Diary of Virginia Woolf*, 10.9.33, ed. Anne Olivier Bell, Vol.4 (London: Hogarth Pr., 1982).

But the greatest Christian art knows and transcends these inadequacies. It knows, and signals the possibility of transcending, the idolatries that bedevil the best religion – the cheap grace, the false hope, the unpurified motive. It comes to have some sense of the cost to God of our redemption – of Christ's role as wounded surgeon ('East Coker') – and hence that the cost to ourselves of the complete simplicity of faith will indeed be 'not less than everything'. This is the achievement of the wartime *Quartets*, and of 'Little Gidding' in particular[4].

'East Coker' pleads for the moment of epiphany not to be isolated, but 'a lifetime burning in every moment', and by the last section of 'The Dry Salvages' Eliot has come through to the conclusion that mystical moments are exceptional, their contemplation a matter for the saint[5], that 'for most of us' the composition of the spiritual life is much more routine. It is a matter of *orientation* towards God, of the attempt to be open to His possibilities. As A.D.Moody shows, Eliot wins through to this with the help of his Indic sources, especially the *Gita*[6]. He modifies Krishna's answer to Arjuna to stress the choice of 'the sphere of being/(on which) the mind of a man may be intent' as 'the one action' which can make an authentic difference to a network of human relationships. This is associated with a kind of death. When the Logos does indeed take its fit place in our language and perceptions then we 'die with the dying'. This is in turn necessarily bound up for the Christian with the Crucifixion. Insofar as we participate in the newness of life offered by the Risen Christ, we share also in his sacrificial death, and do so not for specific gains ('works'), but because that is the character of the life of grace into which the believer is called[7].

There is another sense in which we may understand this question of the sphere of being on which the Christian's mind may be intent. The sense of place, so strong in the openings of the first three *Quartets*, is transmuted

---

4. As Helen Gardner chronicles in her *The Composition of Four Quartets* (London: Faber & Faber, 1978), the last *Quartet* came not 'with practised ease and naturalness', as Bottum states, but after great struggle.

5. Paul Murray helps us here when he directs our attention to Kierkegaard's anti-mystical passage in *Either/Or*, and to Eliot's reference to Kierkegaard in his cancelled Italian lectures of 1939 [*T.S.Eliot and Mysticism*, (Basingstoke: Macmillan, 1991, pp112-4)]. Kierkegaard makes a strong attack on dependence on the mystical moment. He stresses the believer's need to 'choose himself ethically'.

6. See Moody's *Tracing T.S.Eliot's Spirit* (Cambridge: CUP, 1996), Ch.2.

7. Moody links this spiritual attitude also with the Annunciation, in which Mary, the archetypal respondent to God, hears the angel's word, and from her 'Be it unto me according to thy word' (Luke 1.38 AV) comes 'the conceiving of the Word of the Christian revelation'. (Moody, *'Tracing...'*, p29.)

in 'Little Gidding' into 'places/Which are the world's end'. In the lyric that follows the physical elements themselves meet their deaths. In the last analysis of the things of the spirit there is no resting-place (beyond, in a minimal sense, the place of one's own burial). There is only the soul's orientation towards or away from God. For Eliot this was seminally evoked in Dante's famous passage about Arnaut Daniel, after his appeal '*Sovegna Vos*', turning back into the refining fire. Indeed the whole *Purgatorio* depicts this training in the soul's orientation. But its need is seen even more directly in the words of Jesus himself: 'Foxes have holes, and birds of the air have nests; but the Son of Man has nowhere to lay his head' (Luke 9.58, Matthew 8.20 NRSV). The perfectly aware human being has nothing and nowhere but his or her dependence on God. This abstraction from physical place is not 'indifference' but must, after the example of Jesus, 'fructify in the lives of others'. Thus are motives most truly purified 'in the ground of our beseeching'. In 'Little Gidding' mystic delight is no longer looked for; if it is 'half-heard' it is heard from a state of simplicity costing *everything*.

David Daiches suggests five strategies for the religious poet[8]. He/she may: address God, tell the reader about God, recount a visionary experience, find God through the workings of nature, or lastly agonize about God's existence. The *Divina Commedia* in his opinion alternates 'in a most remarkable way between the visionary and the almost pedantically explanatory'. And so too *Four Quartets*, though being written in the age of Russell and Wittgenstein rather than that of Aquinas, Eliot's sequence approaches its religious task in a profoundly oblique way. The word 'God', in any sense that could refer to the Christian God, occurs only twice in the work's 876 lines; Krishna is mentioned as often. The *Quartets*' meditations on 'the intersection of the timeless with time' (which is the essence of revelation, of providence, and of redemption) win through only very gradually to any sustained use of Christian language[9]. The many-layered tracings have the effect of drawing the reader down into a state where, at last, in the final sections of 'Little Gidding' the method of Dante can be followed – we can hear the visionary conclusions of Julian and the author of *The Cloud of Unknowing* cast into the inexorability of sin and the ambiguity of history, and accept that for all their fragility these conclusions will prevail.

8. *God and the Poets* (Oxford: OUP, 1985 edn, Ch.4).
9. See Cleo McNelly Kearns: 'There can be no full unmediated presence of word and thing on the same page, no moment of complete logocentric redemption – at least within time – but only a pointing forward or backward to an elsewhere in which they might possibly intersect. It is perhaps for this reason that Eliot almost never uses either the name of God or even that of Christ in either his poetry or his prose' (*Words in Time*, ed. Lobb, p141).

I come next to a suggestion far more subtle and considered than that of Bottum. This is Moody's suggestion at the end of his essay 'Being in fear of women'[10]: not that Eliot never believed in God, but that he never truly *loved* God, the proof being his failure consistently to love the other human beings closest to him. Therefore, Moody claims, his spiritual explorations do not disclose to us anything fundamental about the nature of Being in general, as opposed to Eliot's particular, strange way of being (which the poet's work so powerfully explores).

This charge derives from an analysis of Eliot's treatment of women both in real life and in three of his later plays (*The Family Reunion*, *The Cocktail Party* and *The Elder Statesman*). Like Craig Raine's assessment of the impact of proven anti-Semitism on Eliot's literary achievement, Moody's verdict on Eliot's *spiritual* state is an exaggeration. Eliot was tremendously aware not only of fear (on which Moody dwells in his essay) but of guilt in respect of women and of God. His faith, falling short of that of a saint, was much concerned with the continual sense of failure which is so integral a part of the penitential tradition in Christianity. Perhaps Moody is right that only at the end of his life did Eliot experience in himself or others that perfect love that 'casts out fear'. But his later poetry nevertheless succeeds in showing us true and false directions in which to search for it[11]. The best of the fruit of his spiritual life, 'by which we may know' him, and hence, however indirectly, something of his God, was first of all in the poetry, also, over time, in his service to the Anglican Church, in personal and professional kindnesses, and finally - this is not to be belittled - in his marital love with Valerie. She has declared him to have been, at that stage of his life, 'made for marriage'[12]. The very considerable strains of the enormous age-gap between them seem never to have been an issue. He gave her a gift of 'six days short of eight years'[13], a gift of great happiness enormously treasured.

The Christian is entitled to ask where authentic happiness is deemed to come *from*, if not from God. Eliot's writing on the spiritual life was not principally about *attainment*, about saintly states directly eloquent of the divine

---

10. In *'Tracing...'*, pp182-95, see also xvii.
11. As Denis Donoghue realised, 'the poems indicate not positions reached but the reaching of positions' [in Bergonzi, Bernard (ed.), *T.S.Eliot: Four Quartets* (London: Macmillan Casebook Series, 1969) p213]. A fascinating letter of Eliot's to William Force Stead on 9.8.30 [quoted by Murray ('..*Mysticism*..' p228)] suggests that it was this poetry of search, rather than devotional verse as such, which particularly concerned him.
12. Interview in *The Independent on Sunday*, 24.4.94.
13. Mrs Eliot's own description, quoted by Lyndall Gordon in *The Craft of Literary Biography*, ed. Jeffrey Meyers (London: Macmillan, 1985), pp173-85.

love. It was about a striving for a certain orientation ('marking channels for others'). His own striving was ultimately rewarded by a gift of love, given and received, so improbable as to be near miraculous. This gift was *not* accompanied by the making of great poetry - the time of searching, and of fruit expressed in the artistic struggle, was over. But the eight-year marriage, like the underlying movement of the *Quartets*, is a profound sign of a sustained belief in love, and love as deriving from, and vindicated by, God.

I have a personal reason for supposing that *Four Quartets* is indeed revelatory of something of the nature of God. My first reading of the poems, plucked by chance off a friend's bookshelf while I was still a science student at Cambridge (and a confirmed agnostic), led me to something very near to a conversion experience. I found the *Quartets* wonderfully eloquent of a new, unfamiliar sort of hope which might stem from a life lived in belief. They were realistic as to the struggle and paradox of aspiration to faith. They left space and silence around 'the drawing of this Love and the voice of this Calling'. I was impoverished by my own failure to respond.

In my first essay I made playful mention of parallels between Eliot and Paul of Tarsus. The personality types, I suspect, were completely different. Nor would even the most uncritical admirer of Eliot claim for him a contribution to the Christian Gospel comparable with that of Paul[14]. But the similarities *are* amusing: both were men of piercing, radical intellectual and rhetorical gifts, and instinctive conservatives strongly committed to the tradition that had formed them. Both were prominent in the 'schools' in which they developed - Paul as a Pharisee, Eliot as a Modernist. Both underwent a conversion astonishing to very many around them[15], but which could later be seen to be in continuity with long spiritual search. Both continued, after their conversion, to show in their profoundly influential writings occasional alarming intolerance, so that those writings are both an inspiration to very many and a real affront to some (e.g. Paul's teachings on women in 1.Cor.11, and on homosexuality in Rom.1 - Eliot's 'Burbank' and *After Strange Gods*). Both experienced intense personal suffering. It is questionable if either ever understood women. Both died with their vision

14. Though Rowan Williams, perhaps surprisingly, describes Eliot as 'a great preacher of the Gospel' [*Open to Judgment*, (London: Darton, Longman & Todd) p219]. And since drawing this parallel I have been amused to discover Stead writing of Eliot that 'he deserved to be reckoned an Apostle to the Gentiles' (*Alumni Journal of Trinity College, XXXVIII*, Winter 1965, No.2, pp59-66).
15. Virginia Woolf wrote to Vanessa Bell that 'Eliot..may be called dead to us all from this day forward. He has become an Anglo-Catholic.' (11.2.28 - *Letters..*, Vol.3, London: Hogarth Pr., 1977). On Paul's conversion see E.P.Sanders, e.g. his *Paul* (Oxford: OUP, 1991).

for a new type of society seemingly doomed to failure. Paul's Church remained weak and scattered at his death in the 60s; Eliot's vision of a new Christendom seems very far from 1990s Britain (though not quite so far from Alasdair MacIntyre's celebrated call for a new St Benedict[16]).

Of course the parallels break down at very many points, not least because Paul's surviving writing forms part of a closed Scriptural canon (though within the informal canon of modern Christian spiritual writing *Four Quartets* has a very central place). But the comparison may be helpful at least in this - that in these times of revisionism in Eliot studies the poet can be seen, like the Apostle, as a very complex child of his time, and judged by the finest of what he wrote as well as the most problematic[17].

The epitaph Thomas Stearns Eliot drafted for himself is understated and seems to imply uncompleted search (see Section VII of 'A Love and its Sounding'). But he had written a more fitting one when he wrote these phrases about Paul Elmer More (a man to whom Eliot claimed uncanny similarity of spiritual experience[18]):

> One is always aware of the sincerity, and in the later works the Christian humanity....of the concentrated mind seeking God; still with restless curiosity analyzing the disease and the aberrations of humanity...[19]

To apply this to Eliot at his best is not to deny the times when he failed his Lord and God.

---

16. In the last sentence of his *After Virtue* (London: Duckworth, 1981).
17. It is sometimes forgotten that Paul wrote not only the difficult passages mentioned above but also the hymn to love in 1.Cor. 13.
18. In his last letter to More in January 1937 [quoted in 'The Rare Contact', by B.A.Harries, *Theology 75*, pp136-44 (1972)].
19. *Princeton Alumni Weekly* 5.2.37.

Select Bibliography

Eliot's own work

My principal sources for Eliot's verse were *The Complete Poems and Plays* (1969), augmented by *The Waste Land, Facsimile and Transcript* ed. V.Eliot (1971), and the recent *Inventions of the March Hare, Poems 1909-1917* ed. C.Ricks (1996). Among his prose writings some of the *Selected Essays* (3rd edn 1951) were important, as were *After Strange Gods* (1934), *The Idea of A Christian Society* (1939), *The Use of Poetry and the Use of Criticism* (1933), and *What is a Classic?* (1945). All the above were published by Faber & Faber, London.

Biographical Sources

There is no authorised biography of Eliot. Lyndall Gordon's two literary-biographical studies: *Eliot's Early Years* and *Eliot's New Life* (Oxford: OUP, 1977 and 1988 respectively) are invaluable for their careful study of the twin influences on TSE of spirituality and female friendship – also for their extensive documenting of sources published and unpublished. Peter Ackroyd's *T.S.Eliot* (London, Hamish Hamilton, 1984) is polished but seems somehow distant from its subject. *The Letters of T.S.Eliot*, of which the first volume, *1898-1922*, edited by Valerie Eliot, was published by Faber & Faber in 1988, are typically fairly cautious documents. However subsequent volumes are keenly awaited – the second is due in 1998.

Introductions to Eliot Criticism

Three short books are particularly helpful: Helen Gardner's *The Art of T.S.Eliot* (London: Faber & Faber, 1968), Stephen Spender's *Eliot* in the Fontana Modern Masters series (Glasgow: Collins, 1975) and Ron Tamplin's *A Preface to T.S.Eliot* (London: Longman, 1988). Two rich collections of essays to appear recently are: *The Cambridge Companion to T.S.Eliot*, ed. A.D.Moody (Cambridge: CUP, 1994) and Moody's own *Tracing T.S.Eliot's Spirit* (Cambridge: CUP, 1996). On *Four Quartets* see in particular Helen Gardner's *The Composition of Four Quartets* (London: Faber & Faber, 1978) and – of the vast critical literature – the essays in *Words in Time*, ed. E.Lobb (London: The Athlone Pr., 1993). Julius' *T.S.Eliot, anti-Semitism and literary form* (Cambridge: CUP, 1995) is, for all its polemic, full of ingenuity; it should be read alongside Christopher Ricks' much more restrained but no less insightful *T.S.Eliot and Prejudice* (London: Faber & Faber, 1988).

Other Works Consulted but not cited in the notes included:

Bush, Ronald, *T.S.Eliot* (Oxford: OUP, 1985)
Carpenter, Humphrey, *A Serious Character: The Life of Ezra Pound* (London: Faber & Faber, 1988)
Childs, Donald, *T.S.Eliot, Mystic, Son and Lover* (London: Athlone Pr., 1997)
Crawford, Robert, *The Savage and the City in the Work of T.S.Eliot* (Oxford: Clarendon, 1987)
Edwards, Michael, *Towards a Christian Poetics* (London: Macmillan, 1984)
Evans, Giles, *Wishwood Revisited* (Sussex: Book Guild Ltd, 1991)
Hughes, Ted, *A Dancer to God* (London: Faber & Faber, 1992)
Lee, Hermione, *Virginia Woolf* (London: Chatto & Windus, 1996)
Matthews, T.S., *Great Tom* (London: Weidenfeld & Nicolson, 1974)
Monk, Ray, *Bertrand Russell - The Spirit of Solitude* (London: Cape, 1996)
Nott, Kathleen, *The Emperor's Clothes* (London: Heinemann, 1953)
Phillips, Caroline, *The Religious Quest in the Poetry of T.S.Eliot* (Lewiston: E. Mellen Pr., 1995)
Reibetanz, J., *A Reading of Eliot's Four Quartets* (Ann Arbor: UMI Research Pr., 1983)
Sharpe, Tony, *T.S.Eliot, A Literary Life* (Basingstoke, Macmillan, 1991)
Soldo, John J., *The Tempering of T.S.Eliot*, (Epping: Bowker, 1983)
Tate, Allen (ed.), *T.S.Eliot, The Man and His Work* (London: Chatto & Windus, 1967)

Concordances and Web Sites (as of April 1997): A printed Concordance exists to *The Complete Poems and Plays*, ed. J.L.Dawson et al. (London: Faber & Faber, 1995) - regrettably it does not cover the unpublished elements in the *Facsimile and Transcript* - or yet the early poems in the Ricks edition.

A still more limited concordance (to the American *Collected Poems 1909-62*) exists on the World Wide Web at http://www.missouri.edu/~enggf/tsebase.html; this site also contains information about subscribing to the (interesting but somewhat frenetic) Eliot discussion list. For a full list of Eliot sites see http://www.modcult.brown.edu/people/Scholes/modlist/AtoF.html.

****